Why a
Shoulc
the Bible?

Booklets taken from Questions of Life:

Is There More to Life Than This?

Who Is Jesus?

Why Did Jesus Die?

How Can We Have Faith?

Why and How Do I Pray?

Why and How Should I Read the Bible?

How Does God Guide Us?

The Holy Spirit

How Can I Resist Evil?

Why and How Should I Tell Others?

Does God Heal Today?

What About the Church?

How Can I Make the Most of the Rest of My Life?

Why and How Should I Read the Bible?

NICKY GUMBEL

First published 1993
Revised in 2011
This new edition 2016

10 09 08 07 06 05 04 03 02 01

ISBN: 978 1 909309 62 3

Published by Alpha International
Holy Trinity Brompton
Brompton Road
London SW7 IJA
Email: publications@alpha.org

Illustrated by Charlie Mackesy

Contents

Why and How Should I Read the Bible?

My father had always wanted to visit Russia and when he was seventy-three and I was twenty-one we went on a family trip to the Soviet Union. At the time, Christians were being persecuted there and it was very hard to get hold of Bibles, but I took some Christian literature with me, including some Russian Bibles. While I was there I went to churches and looked for people who seemed to be genuine Christians. (At that time the meetings were often infiltrated by the KGB.)

On one occasion I followed a man, who was in his sixties, down the street after a service. Glancing round to check nobody was there, I went up to him and tapped him on the shoulder. I took out one of my Bibles and handed it to him. For a moment he had an expression of disbelief. Then he took from his pocket a New Testament, which was probably 100 years old, the pages so threadbare they were virtually transparent. When he realised he had received a whole Bible, he was elated. He didn't speak any English, I didn't speak any Russian. We hugged each other and started dancing up and down the street jumping for joy – not something I normally do with someone I have never met, or anyone else for that matter! That man knew that he had in his hands something truly unique.

Why was he so excited? Many today would see the Bible as rather dull, outdated and irrelevant to their lives. Some prominent atheists go further and describe the God of the Bible as an 'evil monster'. Is this true? Is the Bible really something special? How is it unique?

First, it is uniquely popular. It is the world's best seller. It is estimated that over a hundred million copies of the Bible are sold or given away every year and that there is an average of 6.8 Bibles in every American household. The Bible is the best-selling book of all time – outselling all its rivals year in and year out, decade after decade. Gideon's International gives away a Bible every second. The Bible is available, in all or in part, in 2,426 languages.[1] An article in *The Times* was subheaded 'Forget the modern British novelists and TV tie-ins; the Bible is the biggest-selling book every year.' The writer remarked:

> As usual the top seller by several miles was the... Bible. If cumulative sales of the Bible were frankly reflected in bestseller lists, it would be a rare week when anything else would achieve a look in. It is wonderful, weird, or just plain baffling in this increasingly godless age – when the range of books available grows

wider with each passing year – that this one book should go on selling hand over fist, month in, month out... It is estimated that nearly 1.25 million Bibles and Testaments are sold in the UK each year.

The writer ends by saying, '*All* versions of the Bible sell well *all* the time. I asked the Bible Society for an explanation. "Well," I was told disarmingly, "it is such a good book."'

Second, it is uniquely powerful. As the former prime minister Stanley Baldwin said,

> The Bible is a high explosive. But it works in strange ways and no living man can tell or know how that book, in its journey through the world, has startled the individual soul in ten thousand different places into a new life, a new world, a new belief, a new conception, a new faith.[2]

When I read the Bible at university I was gripped by it. It came alive to me as it never had before and I couldn't put it down. This powerful encounter led to me putting my faith in Christ.

Third, it is uniquely precious. The psalmist says, 'the words of God are more precious than gold' (Psalm 19:10). At her coronation the Queen was handed a Bible by the Moderator of the General Assembly of the Church of Scotland, with these words: 'We present you with this book, the most valuable thing that this world affords.'

Hugh Latimer, the sixteenth-century English bishop, once wrote that the books of the Bible should be constantly in our hands, in our eyes, in our ears, in our mouths, but most of all in our hearts. Scripture, he said, 'turns our souls... it comforts, makes glad, cheers, and cherishes our conscience. It is a more excellent jewel or treasure than any gold or precious stone.'[3]

Why is it so popular, so powerful, so precious? Jesus said: 'People do not live on bread alone, but on every word that comes from the mouth of God' (Matthew 4:4). The verb 'comes' is in the present continuous tense and means 'is continually coming out of the mouth of God'. God is continually wanting to communicate with his people and does so, primarily, through the Bible.

God has spoken: revelation

'In the past God spoke... at many times and in various ways, but in these last days he has spoken to us by his Son' (Hebrews 1:1–2). Christianity is a revealed faith. Jesus Christ is God's ultimate revelation.

The main way we know about Jesus is through God's revelation recorded in the Bible. Biblical theology should be the study of this revelation. God has also revealed himself through creation (Romans 1:19–20; Psalm 19). Science is an exploration of God's revelation in creation. (There should be no conflict between science and the Christian faith; rather they complement one another.[4] Albert Einstein once said, 'science without religion is lame, religion without science is blind... in truth a legitimate conflict between religion and science cannot exist.'[5]) God also speaks to people directly by his Spirit: through prophecy, dreams, visions, and through other people. We will look at these in more detail later – especially in the booklet *How Does God Guide Us?*.

Paul wrote of the inspiration of the Scriptures that were available to him: 'All Scripture is God-breathed and is useful for teaching, rebuking, correcting and training in righteousness, so that God's servant may be thoroughly equipped for every good work' (2 Timothy 3:16–17).

The Greek word for 'God-breathed' is *theopneustos*. It is often translated as 'inspired by God', but literally it means 'God-breathed'. The writer is saying that Scripture is God speaking. Of course he used human authors. The Bible was written over a period of 1,500 years by at least forty authors, from a wide variety of backgrounds – kings, scholars, philosophers, fishermen, poets, statesmen, historians and doctors. The Bible is 100 per cent the work of human beings, but it is also 100 per cent inspired by God (just as Jesus is fully human and fully God).

How can that be? This may be a puzzling paradox, but it is not a contradiction. Sir Christopher Wren, the greatest English architect of his time, built St Paul's Cathedral. He started the project when he was forty-four, continuing the work for the next thirty-five years. It was completed in 1711 when he was seventy-nine. Wren built St Paul's Cathedral, yet he never laid a single stone. There were many different builders but there was only one mind, one architect and one inspiration. So it is with the Bible: there were many different writers but only one inspiration – God himself.

It is clear from the Gospels that Jesus viewed the Scriptures as inspired by God. For him, what the Scriptures said, God said (Mark 7:5–13). If Jesus is our Lord, our attitude to the Scriptures should be the same as his. 'Belief in Christ as the supreme revelation of God leads to belief in scriptural inspiration – of the Old Testament by the direct testimony of Jesus and of the New Testament by inference from his testimony.'[6]

This high view of the inspiration of the Bible has been held almost universally by the worldwide church down the ages. The early theologians of the church had this view. Irenaeus (c. AD 130–200) said, 'The Scriptures are perfect.' Likewise, the reformers, for example, Martin Luther, spoke of 'Scripture which has never erred.' Today, the Roman Catholic official view is enshrined in Vatican II: the Scriptures 'written under the inspiration of the Holy Spirit... have God as their author'. Therefore they must be acknowledged as being 'without error'.[7] This also, until the last century, was the view of all Protestant churches throughout the world, and although today it may be questioned and even ridiculed at a rudimentary level, it continues to be held by many fine scholars.

This does not mean that there are no difficulties in the Bible. Even Peter found some of Paul's letters 'hard to understand' (2 Peter 3:16). There are moral and historical difficulties and some apparent contradictions. Some of the difficulties can be explained by the different contexts in which the many different authors were writing over such a substantial period of time. The Bible contains a whole range of literary genres: history, chronicle, narrative, poetry, prophecy, letters, wisdom and apocalyptic literature.

Although some of the apparent contradictions can be explained by differing contexts, others are harder to resolve. This does not mean, however, that it is impossible or that we should abandon our belief in the inspiration of Scripture. Every great doctrine of the Christian faith should stretch our comprehension. For example, it is hard to reconcile the love of God and the suffering in the world. Yet every Christian believes in the love of God and seeks an understanding of the problem of suffering within that framework. I for one have found that as I have wrestled with this issue I have gained a greater understanding both of suffering and of the love of God.

In a similar way, it is important to hold on to the fact that *all* Scripture is inspired by God, even if we cannot immediately resolve every difficulty. If we do, it should transform the way in which we live our lives. When Billy Graham was a young man, several people (among them, there was one called Chuck) started to say to him, 'You can't believe everything in the Bible.' He began to worry about it and started to become very muddled. John Pollock, in his biography of the evangelist, records what happened:

> So I went back and I got my Bible, and I went out in the moonlight. And I got to a stump and put the Bible on the stump, and I knelt down, and I said, 'Oh God; I cannot prove certain things. I cannot answer some of the questions Chuck is raising and some of the other people are raising, but I accept this Book by faith as the Word of God.' I stayed by the stump praying wordlessly, my eyes moist... I had a tremendous sense of God's presence. I had a great peace that the decision I had made was right.[8]

If we accept that the Bible is inspired by God, then its authority must follow from that. If it is God's word, then it must be our supreme authority for what we believe and how we act. For Jesus, it was his supreme authority; above what the church leaders of his time said (eg Mark 7:1–20) and above the opinions of others, however clever they were (eg Mark 12:18–27). Having said that, we must of course give due weight to what church leaders and others say.

As we have seen, 'All Scripture is God-breathed and is useful for teaching, rebuking, correcting and training in righteousness' (2 Timothy 3:16). First, it is our authority for what we believe – and therefore for 'teaching'. It's in the Bible that we find what God says (and what we should, therefore, believe) about suffering, about Jesus, about the cross and the resurrection and so on.

Second, it is our authority for how we act – for 'rebuking', 'correcting' and for 'training in righteousness'. It is here that we find out what is right and wrong in God's eyes – for example, the Ten Commandments have been described as 'a brilliant analysis of the minimum conditions on which a society, a people, a nation can live a sober, righteous and civilised life'.[9]

There are some things that are very clear in the Bible. It tells us how to conduct our day-to-day lives. We find out what God thinks about relationships and family life. We know that the single state can be a high calling (1 Corinthians 7:7), but it is the exception rather than the rule; marriage is the norm (Genesis 2:24). We know that sexual intercourse outside marriage is wrong. We know that it is right to try to get a job if we can. We know that it is right to give and to forgive.

Some people say, 'I don't want this rule book. It is too restrictive – all those rules and regulations. I want to be free. If you live by the Bible, you are not free to enjoy life.' But is that really right? Does the Bible take away our freedom? Or does it in fact give us freedom? Rules and regulations can in fact create freedom and increase our enjoyment of life.

Some years ago, a football match had been arranged involving twenty-two small boys, including one of my sons, aged eight at the time. A friend of mine called Andy (who had been training the boys all year) was going to referee. Unfortunately, by 2.30 pm he had not turned up. The boys could wait no longer. I was press-ganged into being the substitute referee. There were a number of difficulties with this: I had no whistle; there were no markings for the boundaries of the pitch; I didn't know any of the other boys' names; they did not have colours to distinguish which sides they were on; and I did not know the rules nearly as well as some of the boys.

The game soon descended into complete chaos. Some shouted that the ball was in. Others said that it was out. I wasn't at all sure, so I let things run. Then the fouls started. Some cried, 'Foul!' Others said, 'No foul!' I didn't know who was right. So I let them play on. Then people began to get hurt. By the time Andy arrived, there were three boys lying injured on the ground and all the rest were shouting, mainly at me! But the moment Andy arrived, he blew his whistle, arranged the teams, told them where the boundaries were and had them under complete control. Then the boys had the game of their lives.

Were the boys more free without the rules or were they in fact less free? Without any effective authority they were free to do exactly what they wanted. The result was that people were confused and hurt. They much preferred it when they knew where the boundaries were. Then within those boundaries they were free to enjoy the game.

God has given us guidelines on how to live because he loves us and he wants us to enjoy life to the full. God did not say, 'Do not murder,' in order to ruin our enjoyment of life. Nor did he say 'Do not commit adultery,' because he is a spoilsport. He said these things because he did not want people to get hurt. The Bible is God's revelation of his will for all people. The more we live according to his will, the freer we shall be. God has spoken and we need to hear what he has said.

God speaks: relationship

For some people the Bible is never more than a well-thumbed manual for life. They analyse it, read commentaries on it (and there is nothing wrong with that), but we must remember that not only has God spoken, but he still speaks today through what he has said in the Bible. St Gregory the Great said, 'The Bible is a letter from God' and St Augustine: 'The Bible does nothing but speak of God's love for us.'

For most of our married life my wife Pippa and I haven't had to be apart for substantial periods of time. But I remember I once had to be away for three and a half weeks. Each morning at the place I was staying I would rush down and check the hall table for any letters. If I saw her handwriting my heart would leap. Why? Because it was a letter from the person I loved. Similarly the Bible is God's love letter to us.

The main point of the Bible is to show us how to enter into a relationship with God through Jesus Christ. Jesus said, 'You diligently study the Scriptures because you think that by them you possess eternal life. These are the Scriptures that testify about me, yet you refuse to come to me to have life' (John 5:39–40).

To use an analogy, imagine for a moment that I drive an ageing Nissan. This car has served me well and being pleased with it I decide to order a brand new Nissan to be delivered to my home. When it arrives at our front door I go outside and admire it. As I check out the inside of the car, I discover in the glove compartment the Nissan manual. Excited by this find I take the manual inside and start studying it. I then get out my felt-tip pen and begin to underline sections that I like and then to learn them by heart.

I also cut out some sections and stick them to my bathroom mirror so that I can read them while shaving. I even join a club of like-minded manual enthusiasts. There they encourage me to learn Japanese, so that I can study the manual in its original language. Remember this is an analogy! If this were true clearly I would have missed the point; the purpose of the manual is to help us to drive the car. In the same way, it is no good studying the Bible if we miss the point, which is to come into a living relationship with Jesus. Martin Luther said, 'Scripture is the manger or "cradle" in which the infant Jesus lies. Don't let us inspect the cradle and forget to worship the baby.'

Our relationship with God is two-way. We speak to him in prayer and he speaks to us in many ways, but especially through the Bible. God speaks through what he has spoken. The writer of the epistle to the Hebrews says, when he quotes the Old Testament, 'As the Holy Spirit *says*' (Hebrews 3:7). It is not just that the Holy Spirit spoke in the past. He still speaks through what he said in the Bible. This is what makes the Bible so alive. Again, as Martin Luther put it, 'The Bible is alive, it speaks to me; it has feet, it runs after me; it has hands, it lays hold of me.'

What happens when God speaks?

First, he brings faith to those who are not yet Christians. Paul says, 'Faith comes from hearing the message, and the message is heard through the word of Christ' (Romans 10:17). It is often as people read the Bible that they come to faith in Jesus Christ. That was certainly my experience and it has been the experience of many other people.

Actor David Suchet, well-known for his title role in *Poirot*, tells how a few years ago he was lying in his bath in a hotel in America, when he had a sudden and impulsive desire to read the Bible. He managed to find a Gideon Bible and he started to read the New Testament. As he read, he came to put his faith in Jesus Christ. He said:

> From somewhere I got this desire to read the Bible again. That's the most important part of

my conversion. I started with the Acts of the Apostles and then moved to Paul's Letters – Romans and Corinthians. And it was only after that I came to the gospels. In the New Testament I suddenly discovered the way that life should be followed.

Second, he speaks to Christians. As we read the Bible we experience a transforming relationship with God through Jesus Christ. Paul says, 'We, who with unveiled faces all reflect the Lord's glory, are being transformed into his likeness with ever-increasing glory, which comes from the Lord, who is the Spirit' (2 Corinthians 3:18). As we study the Bible, we come into contact with Jesus Christ. It has always struck me as the most extraordinarily wonderful fact that we can speak to and hear from the person whom we read about in the pages of the New Testament – the same Jesus Christ. He will speak to us (not audibly, on the whole, but in our heart) as we read the Bible. We will hear his message for us. As we spend time with him, our characters will become more like his.

Spending time in his presence, listening to his voice, brings many blessings. He often brings joy and peace, even in the middle of a crisis in our lives (Psalm 23:5). When we are not sure which direction we should be going in, God often guides us through his word (Psalm 119:105). The book of Proverbs even tells us that God's words bring healing to our bodies (Proverbs 4:22).

The Bible also provides us with a defence against spiritual attack. We only have one detailed example of Jesus facing temptation. Jesus faced intense attack by the devil at the start of his ministry (Matthew 4:1-11). Jesus met every temptation with a verse from the Scriptures. I find it fascinating that every one of his replies came from Deuteronomy 6–8. It seems plausible to infer that Jesus had been studying this portion of Scripture and that it was fresh in his mind.

The word of God has great power. The writer of the book of Hebrews says, 'The word of God is living and active. Sharper than any double-edged sword, it penetrates even to dividing soul and spirit, joints and marrow; it judges the thoughts and attitudes of the heart' (Hebrews 4:12). It has power to pierce all our defences and get through to our hearts. I remember once reading Philippians 2:4, 'Each of you should look not only to your own interests, but also to the interests of others.' It was like an arrow going straight into me as I realised how selfish I was being. In these, and many other ways, God's word speaks to us.

As God speaks to us and we learn to hear his voice, our relationship with him grows, and our love for him deepens. Rick Warren has written that reading the Bible, 'generates life, creates faith, produces change... heals hurts, builds character, transforms circumstances, imparts joy, overcomes adversity, defeats temptation, infuses hope, releases power [and] cleanses our minds'.[10]

How do we hear God speak through the Bible?

Time is our most valuable possession. The pressure on time tends to increase as life goes on and we become busier and busier. There is a saying that goes 'money is power, but time is life'. If we are going to set aside time to read the Bible, we have to plan ahead. If we don't plan we will never do it. Don't be depressed if you only keep to 80 per cent of your plan. Sometimes we oversleep!

It is wise to start with a realistic goal. Don't be over-ambitious. It is better to spend a few minutes every day than to spend an hour-and-a-half the first day and then to give up. If you have never studied the Bible before, you might like to set aside seven minutes every day. I am sure that if you do that regularly you will steadily increase it.

Mark tells us that Jesus got up early and went off to a *solitary place* to pray (Mark 1:35). It is important to try to find somewhere where we can be on our own. I find that first thing in the morning is the best time. I take a cup of coffee, the Bible, my diary and a notebook. I use the notebook to write down prayers and also things I think God may be saying to me. I use the diary to help me pray about each stage of my day, but also for jotting down any distracting thoughts or plans that come to my mind.

I start by asking God to speak to me through the passage I am reading. Then I read it. It's a good idea to start by reading a few verses of one of the Gospels each day. You might find it helpful to use Bible reading notes, which are available at most Christian bookshops, or perhaps a Bible study website or app, such as the *Bible in One Year*.[11]

As I read, I ask myself three questions:

1. What does it say? I read it at least once and, if necessary, compare different translations.
2. What does it mean? What did it mean to the person who first wrote it and those who first read it? (This is where the notes may be helpful.)
3. How does it apply to me, my family, my work, my neighbours, the society around me? (It is when we see the relevance to our own lives that Bible reading becomes so exciting and we become conscious that we are hearing God's voice.)

Finally, we must put into practice what we hear from God. Jesus said, 'Therefore everyone who hears these words of mine and puts them into practice is like a wise man who built his house on the rock' (Matthew 7:24). As D. L. Moody pointed out, 'The Bible was not given to increase our knowledge. It was given to change lives.'

I would encourage you to develop a regular pattern of reading the Bible each day and praying that God would speak to you. It is an amazing experience when he does. Sometimes reading the Bible can be mundane, but sometimes it is particularly significant. This has certainly been my experience. God spoke to me very clearly about my father after he died in 1981. I had become a Christian seven years earlier and my parents' initial reaction was one of complete horror. Gradually, over the years, they began to see a change in me. My mother became a committed Christian long before she died. My father was a man of few words. Initially, he was very unsure about my involvement in the Christian faith. By degrees, he started to become warmer about it. His death was quite sudden. I missed him dreadfully but what I found hardest about his death was that I wasn't sure whether he was a Christian or not.

Exactly ten days after his death, I was reading the Bible. I had asked God to speak to me about my father that day because I was still worrying about him. I happened to be reading Romans and I came across the verse, 'Everyone who calls on the name of the Lord will be saved' (Romans 10:13). I sensed at that moment God was saying to me that this verse was for my father; that he had called on the name of the Lord and been 'saved'. About five minutes later my wife, Pippa, came in and said to me, 'I have been reading a verse in Acts 2:21 and I think this verse is for your father. It says, "… and everyone who calls on the name of the Lord will be saved."' It was quite extraordinary because that verse only appears twice in the New Testament and God had spoken to both of us through the same words at the same time in different parts of the Bible.

Three days later, we went to a Bible study in a friend's home and the Bible study was on Romans 10:13, that same passage. So three times during those three days God spoke to me about my father through the same words. Nevertheless, on my way to work I was still thinking about my father and worrying about him. As I came out of the Underground, I looked up and there was a huge poster saying, 'Whoever calls upon the name of the Lord will be saved' (Romans 10:13). I remember talking to a friend about it and telling him what had happened. He said to me, 'Do you think the Lord may be trying to speak to you?'

Endnotes

1. See John Micklethwait and Adrian Wooldridge, *God is Back: How the Global Rise of Faith is Changing the World* (Allen Lane, 2009), pp.177 and 266.
2. Stanley Baldwin, *This Torch of Freedom* (Ayer Publishing, 1971), p.92.
3. Quoted in Alister McGrath's Commemorative Lecture to the Latimer Trust, 2005.
4. For further reading on this subject, please see Nicky Gumbel, *Searching Issues* (Alpha International, 2016) and *Is God a Delusion?* (Alpha International, 2008).
5. Albert Einstein, *Ideas and Opinions* (Crown Publishers, Inc., 1954).
6. John W. Wenham, *Christ and the Bible* (Tyndale: USA, 1972).
7. *Dei Verbum*, Chapter 3, 11.
8. John Pollock, *Billy Graham: The Authorised Biography* (Hodder & Stoughton, 1966).
9. Bishop Stephen Neill, *The Supremacy of Jesus* (Hodder & Stoughton, 1984).
10. Rick Warren, *The Purpose-Driven Life* (Zondervan, 2002), p.186.
11. To help start reading the Bible, please see Nicky Gumbel, *30 Days* (Alpha International, 2012) or download a Bible reading app, such as *Bible in One Year* (bibleinoneyear.org) written by Nicky and Pippa Gumbel, or other Bible reading plans, such as the YouVersion Bible app.

Alpha

Alpha is a practical introduction to the Christian faith, initiated by HTB in London and now being run by thousands of churches, of many denominations, throughout the world. If you are interested in finding out more about the Christian faith and would like details of your nearest Alpha, please visit our website:

alpha.org

or contact:
The Alpha Office,
HTB Brompton Road,
London,
SW7 1JA

Tel: 0845 644 7544

Alpha titles available

Why Jesus?   A booklet – given to all participants at the start of Alpha. 'The clearest, best illustrated and most challenging short presentation of Jesus that I know.' – Michael Green

Why Christmas?   The Christmas version of *Why Jesus?*

Questions of Life   Alpha in book form. In fifteen compelling chapters Nicky Gumbel points the way to an authentic Christianity which is exciting and relevant to today's world.

Searching Issues   The seven issues most often raised by participants on Alpha, including, suffering, other religions, science and Christianity, and the Trinity.

A Life Worth Living   What happens after Alpha? Based on the book of Philippians, this is an invaluable next step for those who have just completed Alpha, and for anyone eager to put their faith on a firm biblical footing.

The Jesus Lifestyle Studies in the Sermon on the Mount showing how Jesus' teaching flies in the face of a modern lifestyle and presents us with a radical alternative.

30 Days Nicky Gumbel selects thirty passages from the Old and New Testament which can be read over thirty days. It is designed for those on Alpha and others who are interested in beginning to explore the Bible.

All titles are by Nicky Gumbel,
who is vicar of Holy Trinity Brompton

About the Author

Nicky Gumbel is the pioneer of Alpha. He read law at Cambridge and theology at Oxford, practised as a barrister and is now vicar of HTB in London. He is the author of many bestselling books about the Christian faith, including *Questions of Life*, *The Jesus Lifestyle*, *Why Jesus?*, *A Life Worth Living*, *Searching Issues* and *30 Days*.